Do You Really Want To Be Healed?

Do You Really Want To Be Healed?

Desmond Hynes

BEST WISHES
WITH
LOVE AND COMPASSION
DES HYNES

Stellium Ltd

Published in 2015 by Stellium Ltd
22 Second Avenue, Camels Head
Plymouth, Devon PL2 2EQ UK
www.stelliumpub.com   email: stelliumpub@gmail.com
Desmond Hynes has asserted his moral right
to be identified as the author of this work in terms of
the Copyright, Designs and Patents Act 1988
British Library Cataloguing-in-Publication Data:
A catalogue record for this book is available from
the British Library
Copyright © 2015 Desmond Hynes
Cover design: © 2015 Jan Budkowski
Typeset by Zambezi Publishing Ltd, Plymouth UK
Printed and bound in the UK by Lightning Source (UK) Ltd
ISBN: 978-0-9575783-6-4

About the Author

Des Hynes is an Usui/Holy Reiki Master and Teacher, and he is a member of The UK Reiki Federation.

He was born in Dublin in 1950, and after leaving school at the age of fourteen with no qualifications, he started work in a factory assembling Morris Minor motor cars. Two years later at the age of sixteen, he started an apprenticeship as a barman in a Dublin pub, which led to him working in some of the most deprived areas of the city.

His desire to travel began when he joined the Royal Navy at the age of twenty, and over the next thirty years, this took him to many places, including Tokyo, Hong Kong, Seattle, New York, San Diego, Mexico, Canada, India, Alaska, Kenya, Ukraine, Somalia, South Korea, Malaysia, Israel, Jordan, Libya, Algeria, East Germany (just after the wall came down), Bermuda and Jamaica.

Des once sailed around the world the wrong way (going East through the Suez Canal and returning through the Panama Canal), and thus gained a complete day. He says that when the time comes, he can put his age plus one day on his grave stone - unless he goes around the world the right way before he dies, that is!

After thirty years in the Navy, Des settled down in Plymouth with his wife Vivienne and two children,

Kevin and Jennifer. It was while Vivienne was being treated for cancer that he became interested in Reiki, as he could see the benefit that the healing energy bestowed upon her, and the way that it combatted the side effects of the chemotherapy. He believes that even though his wife passed away four years after being diagnosed, the Reiki had helped her and it also helped others who were coping with the cancer treatment.

July 2015

Dedication

To the memory of

Vivienne Barbara Hynes

1952 - 2013

Contents

Chapter 1: Introduction to the Subject 1

Chapter 2: What Causes Illness? 5

Chapter 3: Energy 11

Chapter 4: The Chakras and Auras 14

Chapter 5: Understanding the Techniques 18

Chapter 6: Healing the Past 24

Chapter 7: Reiki, or Energy Healing 28

Chapter 8: Other Forms of Holistic Healing . . .32

Index 38

Contents

Chapter 1:
Introduction to the Subject

This book is written from a holistic viewpoint. I do not and am not in a position to offer a medical opinion and I do not suggest you disregard your doctor's advice. I am a Reiki Master and healer and have seen the benefits of Reiki healing when used in conjunction with traditional medicine. Reiki is offered to patients in some hospitals to help with the side effects of chemotherapy treatment for cancer.

I believe medicine on its own does not have the power to heal, as it is also the power of the mind that facilitates healing. Those who put all their confidence in medicine weaken their minds and find they become dependent on medicine. Thinking positive thoughts, prayers, affirmations, visualization and cheerfulness stimulates the natural healing process of the body.

Reiki is a Japanese technique for Stress Reduction and Relaxation that also promotes healing. It was rediscovered by Dr. Mikao Usui in the early 1990s. It is said that while he was teaching in a Christian seminary in Japan, one of his students asked him if he believed in the Bible stories about Jesus healing, and if so, when they were going to be taught to heal. It was then that

Do You Really Want To Be Healed?

Dr Usui started his search to find the answer to this question, starting with research of both Christian and Buddhist sacred texts. He went to a place called Mount Kurama, where he fasted and meditated. After twenty-one days, he had a "satori" which is the Japanese word traditionally meaning "One who has a fleeting glimpse or understanding of a higher order". We say that Dr Mikao *rediscovered* the method of healing, because it had always been there.

"Do you really want to be healed?" might seem a strange question to ask someone who is ill, because the majority of people will answer, "Yes of course I want to be healed." But how many times do you see hospital patients in their dressing gowns standing outside the hospital entrance, connected to all their life saving equipment, smoking a cigarette? They have been told that smoking is bad for them, but they still carry on. Also, the alcoholic who has had a liver transplant and continues to drink. I am sure that they believe that they want to live a healthy life, but they have subconsciously become attached to their illness.

There may be many reasons why someone can't let go of this attachment. They might have grown to accept it, or, strange though it may seem, they might be afraid of the responsibility that will come with perfect health. As a Reiki Healer, I have come across people who are afraid to be healed. Our society, with its free and available health care and its generous disability support system, can subconsciously be an obstacle for some people wanting change. This does not mean we should scrap the disability payments to people and their families who rely on the money to live a comfortable and secure existence, but the

Introduction to the Subject

continued illness might also be a way of getting affection from loved ones. (We know how we fuss over our children when they are unwell). All of these reasons may be in the subconscious.

When we visit the doctor, we feel cheated if we don't come away with a prescription for some form of medication, because we want to get our money's worth. We have become a nation of hypochondriacs. A survey in England in 2013 showed that 50 per cent of the adult population take regular prescription drugs; cholesterol-lowering statins, pain relief and anti-depressants were among the most prescribed drugs. The cost to the NHS was £15 billion a year, and that is just for England. Conventional medicine only treats the symptoms of the illness. Do you want to be reliant on the large pharmaceutical companies for your future well-being?

The Holistic approach treats the cause of illness in the Body, Mind or Soul. In ancient China, the village doctor got paid to prevent illness, so if nobody got ill he was doing his job well, but if too many people got sick, he got sacked. How would you feel if your doctor told you to rest, stop eating for twenty-four hours and drink plenty of water? When we are ill we lose our appetite; this is a message from our body telling us to give our digestive system a chance to rest. Our body uses energy to turn the food we eat into fuel to sustain life, but by resting the process of digestion, this energy can be redirected to help with the natural healing abilities that we all have in us. We are equipped with amazing and sophisticated healing processes that allow our bodies to repair and maintain themselves if we allow them to do so. New research

Do You Really Want To Be Healed?

has shown that 98 per cent of the cells in our body are renewed each year. Your liver gradually replaces itself every six weeks, your skin is renewed every month and your stomach lining every four days. Many things can have an effect on this natural regeneration. We need to eat a healthy, balanced diet and drink plenty of water. We also need to get enough sleep and avoid stress.

*"Those that put all their confidence in drugs
weaken their minds, and find
they become dependent on drugs"*

Chapter 2:
What Causes Illness?

Stress

I believe the biggest contribution to ill health is stress. What causes Stress? Two of the main contributions to Stress are Anger and Worry.

Anger + Worry = Stress = Illness

Anger

As part of the Reiki practitioner's code, there are five principles that we recite at least once a day, normally first thing in the morning. One of those principles is: "*Just For Today, I Will Let Go of Anger.*" Note how we say "just for today". We are only promising to ourselves that it is just for today we will let go of Anger.

We get angry when people or things don't meet our expectations. Sometimes we can get angry with ourselves if we don't come up to the standards that we set ourselves. It is also common for us to get

Do You Really Want To Be Healed?

angry with those we care about the most. Anger is a very destructive emotion that can create serious blockages in our energy field. It is the most complex inner enemy. You hear stories about families that have fallen out and not spoken to each other for years, and as time goes by, the original reason for the conflict becomes obscure. We mistakenly think of being angry as having power over others, but the reverse is true - it clouds our judgement and makes us weak. Anger is a conscious choice, a habitual response we have developed, and it is why everyone responds differently to similar situations.

I treated a man who was developing an uncontrollable shaking in his hands. He had all the tests and could find no medical reason why this should have started, so as a last resort he came to me for a Reiki treatment. During the Reiki session, I noticed a blockage in the Solar Plexus Chakra, so at the end of the treatment, I asked him if he was worried or got angry, and he confirmed that he was under medication for anger issues.

Sometimes we have anger issues when we lose control of things. For example, the man who loses his job may have to come to terms with his wife being the main breadwinner in the family, or someone who is ill gets angry because he cannot support his family. The best way to break this habitual response to anger is by practising meditation and receiving some Reiki healing. Try spending time in nature. A walk in the woods or a stroll along the beach with the waves lapping around your feet will help. This way, you connect with the energy that is so important for our well-being.

What Causes Illness?

Some of you will say, my life is so busy I never have the time to do these things – but it is up to you to make time. If you don't make the time now, you will have plenty of time later when you are ill in hospital.

Another suggestion is to plug yourself into your personal CD or iPod player during the evening when everyone else is watching some old soap on television. Stop watching soaps on television, live your own life rather than that of some sad character on the box. Reality is much more exciting.

Worry

Another Reiki principle is: "*Just for Today, I Will Let Go of Worry.*" While anger deals with past and present events, worry deals with future ones. Although worry is not always a negative phenomenon, endless worries may fill one's head, and each one bores a small hole in one's body and soul.

Can you remember what you were worried about this time last year or this time five years ago? Worry is the fear of "What if". We worry about:

- What if I lose my job?
- What if I get ill?
- What if I marry the wrong person?
- Will the car break down?
- Will the roof leak?

Worrying about these things will not make any difference. Nine out of the ten things we worry about never

Do You Really Want To Be Healed?

happen. It is a bad habit that we get into, and like any bad habit, we can get rid of it. We also worry about the ones we love, but to worry about someone else is a waste of our time and energy. We can advise and support people, but we have to realise that each one of us is a free spirit and we all have free will and we can all choose for ourselves – after all, that principle started in the Garden of Eden when Adam ate the apple.

When we worry, we get depressed, go to the doctor and end up with anti-depression pills. How many people carry on taking the medication even when they don't need it? We suppress this negative emotion instead of getting rid of it. Reiki and meditation can help break the negative habit of worry. Some of us are natural worriers. There are only two days you can do nothing about, one is yesterday and the other is tomorrow. To live we need food, clothing and shelter, so anything else is a bonus. Have we come to expect too much? Do we forget what we have? Just because someone has a big house with a swimming pool and a posh car does not mean they are happy. There are a lot of unhappy rich people as well as poor people.

When I was a child growing up in Dublin in the early 1950s, we were all poor. There was no peer pressure to have better things, we were just happy to have a roof over our heads and something to eat. Certain things from your childhood will always remain in your mind. One of the saddest things I remember from that time was when I was walking past our local pub at about seven o'clock one dark evening, and parked outside was a Morris Traveller motor car that had a child's coffin with a bunch of flowers on top of it in the back of the car. I imagine

What Causes Illness?

that the people were too late to get to the cemetery so went to the pub instead.

Psychological Problems

While a physical illness is easy to see, the psychological illnesses that people suffer are less evident. These can result in depression, anxiety and isolation. When we are children, the first seven years of our life is the time when our Root/Base Chakra is opening and developing. This is the time when we most need the love and support of our parents and extended family. We need to know that we are wanted and protected. From the age of seven to fourteen years, our Sacral Chakra starts to open, and we learn to experience the world through our feelings and emotions. It is then that we learn to decide what experiences are nice and good, and which are ugly and painful. It is in the latter stage of this opening that puberty occurs.

The child is at a very susceptible stage when the first two chakras are opening; any harmful influences that occur at this time can be carried into adulthood. For instance, if the mother and father are in a relationship of conflict, and if the mother has no respect for her husband, she may say to the young boy, "You are just like your father, and you won't amount to anything when you grow up!" If this is drummed in, a seed plants itself in the child's subconscious mind that grows and ultimately undermines his belief in his own self-worth. How many times have you seen young boys and girls becoming mini versions of their parents?

Do You Really Want To Be Healed?

When we were young, our expectations were set by what we were told we would be. I remember when I was a child, being asked what I wanted to be when I grew up, and I replied that I wanted to be a coal delivery man with a horse and cart, so that I could give my mother free coal, so we would always have a fire in the winter. This might seem lacking in ambition, but at that time, having enough coal to keep the fire going was an important part of the family's survival. Also, the coal man was strong from carrying those bags of coal, all of which denotes that my subconscious was being directed towards the basic survival needs that are indicative of the Root/Base Chakra.

Sometimes there is a cycle that repeats itself. If the parents suffered physical or mental abuse as children, they in turn may become the abusers. It is also the case that some parents try to relive their own lives through their children instead of allowing them to exercise free will. This type of control over others is harmful to both parties. When the child reaches middle age, he or she can look back and see the lost opportunities, and this can lead to resentment and unhappiness. With Reiki healing, it is possible to break this cycle of control. It is a fact that we can advise and offer support to others, but in the end, we are all free spirits and we all have free will.

Chapter 3:
Energy

There is energy in everything, from stones and plants to animals and humans, although the energy in a rock vibrates at a different frequency to the energy in a human. We are all comprised of electromagnetic energy that flows through every cell and atom that makes up the human body. This Energy is known by different names: *Ki* in Japan, *Chi* in China and *Prana* in India respectively. Reiki is made up of two words, *Rei-Ki* (pronounced Ray Kee). The first part *Rei* means universal or divine, higher wisdom. The second part *Ki* means the life force energy that flows through all things.

So, we are surrounded with this universal life force energy that sustains life as we know it. We can pick on other people's energy through their auras. Young children and animals are good at picking up energy from people's auras, because children use the gift of their instincts. We are all born with these instincts, but as we get older, we allow logic and mistrust to replace them. How many times have you met someone for the first time and instinctively liked or disliked them? Sometimes, even before you enter a room, you can sense the atmosphere on the other side of the door. Places can also maintain the energy of those who lived in them or frequented them. It's like going into a pub in a strange town, where the way you feel when you walk in decides whether you stay for one drink or sit around until closing time.

This reminds me of an experience that I had during my long service career in the Royal Navy. The ship had docked in New York, and it was late at night when my mate Taff and I decided to go into a certain pub for a drink. When we stepped inside, there was a deadly silence from the packed bar, and it was only when we ordered our drinks that we realised that we were the only two white people in the room. Once the cliental realised that we were not locals but visitors to their city from Ireland and Wales, the atmosphere changed completely, and we were made to feel as if that bar was our local.

People are the same all over the world. If you send out positive, loving energy vibrations, you get the same coming back. As we move into the Age of Aquarius, there will be a growth in, and the acceptance of, holistic treatments like Reiki and Acupuncture. We will rediscover ancient ways of healing from within.

As I have already mentioned, there is energy / Ki within and all around us. At the earth's core, there is a large crystal that emits energy, and from outside the earth in the cosmos, the energy flows down on us. When we ground ourselves, we connect to the earth by imagining roots coming out of the soles of our feet and working their way down to the crystal that sits in the centre of our planet. It is important to be grounded, because we live in a physical world and we need that connection to carry out our everyday tasks. With practice, we can direct Ki to specific parts of our body. This is helpful when we need Ki to be concentrated in an area that is making us feel ill – for example, to the head if we have a hangover, or the belly if we have over indulged. If we direct our Ki to the upper part of our body, we become lighter, and if it is directed to the lower part, we become heavier. How many times have you seen a mother struggling when trying to lift a child if that child does not want to do something? Martial arts masters who practice controlling their Ki can make themselves so heavy and rooted that when as many as four people try to lift them up, they can't do it. It can be exciting directing your Ki to various parts of your own body, simply by means of the power of your thoughts.

When I give a Reiki healing, I ground myself to the earth by imagining roots coming from the soles of my feet and travelling down through the earth, then I open my Crown Chakra to accept the flow of universal energy from above. The Ki flows down to my Heart Chakra, then down my arms till it reaches the palms of my hands. By laying my hands on, or close to, the person receiving the healing, the Ki flows into them. This is the way I carry out healing using the direct contact method of healing with the patient. (There is also a distant healing method of Reiki where the person being healed does not have to be present). After the Reiki sessions, I have to make sure the recipient of the Reiki is fully grounded and back in the physical world before he or she leaves, as the world would not be a safe place if my clients drove around with their heads in the clouds!

Chapter 4:
The Chakras and Auras

Chakra is a Sanskrit word meaning "wheel" and it refers to each of the seven centres of your energy system, which are the pumps or valves that allow the energy to flow smoothly. The energy of each Chakra vibrates at a different frequency in relation to the other chakras. The heaviest or densest is at the lowest (Root/Base Chakra) and the lightest is at the top (Crown Chakra).

The seven main chakras are:

- The Root or Base
- Sacral
- Solar plexus
- Heart
- Throat
- Third Eye
- Crown

Note: Some people use different names for some of the Chakras, so you may know the Solar Plexus Chakra as the Spleen Chakra, and the Third Eye Chakra as the Brow Chakra.

The Chakras and Auras

Each of the Chakras serves a different purpose, for example the Root Chakra, which is situated at the base of the spine, is where we connect to our basic survival instincts, such as where to shelter, what to eat and how to keep warm. At the other end of the scale, we have the Crown Chakra, which is situated at the Crown of the head, and this is associated with spiritual knowledge and the connection with our higher self. We associate the lower Chakras with the practical aspects of our life, so the Root/Base Chakra relates to survival instincts, the Sacral Chakra is associated with emotions and sexuality, and the Solar Plexus Chakra is where we feel power and self-esteem.

When we meditate, we tend to use the Chakras on the upper part of our bodies, because this is where we connect to our spiritual or higher self. The Heart Chakra is concerned with love and compassion, and the Throat Chakra relates to communication and clairaudience. The Third Eye Chakra is used for clairvoyance and intuition, and the Crown Chakra is for divine guidance.

In healing, we use the Meridian system, which is a network of invisible channels that facilitate the flow of Ki around the body along with the Chakras, so it is essential for the health and harmony of our mind, body and soul that the Chakras are working in harmony. When we are balanced, all the Chakras are open and there is an uninterrupted flow of energy within and around our bodies. When there is a blockage or reversal in one or more of the Chakras, it can result in illness. The Reiki healer clears this blockage and restores the flow of Ki.

Do You Really Want To Be Healed?

The Auras

The Aura is an electromagnetic field that surrounds the human body. Some people can see auras as colours, but most people can only feel or sense them.

The first Aura is close to the physical body, and it is called the "Physical Auric Body". It is associated with physical sensations and comfort. This aura extends from one quarter to two inches beyond the physical body.

The second Aura layer is the "Etheric Auric Body", and this is not as dense as the first layer. It is associated with feelings such as love, excitement, joy or anger, and it extends between one to three inches from the body.

The third Aura layer is "The Vital Auric Body", and this extends beyond the Etheric layer and is finer in density. This is where our rational mind and thought forms can be observed. If we are angry, this aura glows with red colours, and if we are happy, it shows yellow or gold. These first three layers are connected to the physical plane.

The fourth Aura layer is "The Astral Level", and it is at this level where we interact with other people. For instance, we can communicate our feeling to someone to whom we are attracted through this level. This where the energy fields of two people who are compatible talk to each other. This level extends from six inches to one foot from the body.

The final Aura layer bridges the physical plane and

The Chakras and Auras

the spiritual plane and it is called "The Lower Mental / Divine Level".

*"Spend time with Nature, and
absorb the Energy"*

Chapter 5:
Understanding the Techniques

Meditation

Meditation is a central part of several religions, but it can also be practised by non-believers. By using meditation, we clear our minds of unwanted thoughts and worries and we achieve self-awareness. There are many different methods of meditation: Christian meditation includes quietly praying or just contemplating the love of Christ for oneself and for mankind. You don't have to sit in the Lotus position and chant mantras to meditate. Just sit upright in a comfortable chair and clear your mind of all thoughts for half an hour, and that should do the trick. When you start to meditate you might find it hard to clear your mind, but there are many ways to achieve this. For instance, take three deep breaths and concentrate on the in breath and then the out breath.

Different people use various techniques to meditate; these range from chanting, which leads to a hypnotic state that clears the mind, other people like to listen to music and burn incense, while yet others prefer silence when mediating. There are various exercises that can be employed to help focus the mind. To fill

Understanding the Techniques

ourselves with universal love, we have to first empty the cup. Once we clear our minds, we can start to put positive and healing thoughts in, so there are affirmations we can repeat. For example, for healing you could say, *"My real self is happy and perfect, and illness is an illusion."* Repeat this phrase to yourself several times and believe it, because it is true. Visualization is also a powerful tool for healing.

Visualization

The root cause of stress is in our minds, and we develop anger and worry though negative thoughts. Don't underestimate the power of your thoughts; they can be used to heal as well as do harm. We tend to use our intellect far more than our imagination or intuition. In the esoteric traditions of the Far East, there is a belief that our physical world is an illusion behind which exists a "Greater Reality", but we only accept what we can touch, taste, see or smell. We have to realise that *there is no solid matter*: it is only energy moving at such a low frequency that gives it the illusion of form.

This reminds me of the time I spent in the Navy as a Stoker Petty Officer. The boilers we steamed used water that was heated and turned into saturated steam (wet steam) then recycled within the boiler and heated to a further 850 degrees Fahrenheit, which became superheated steam (dry steam). It was very dangerous, because if there was a leak you could not see it, but it was this steam that was used to turn turbines of some of the auxiliary machinery and the main engines. So within the boiler, something that had been visible was transformed into something invisible but even more powerful.

When we accept that there are worlds existing at subatomic levels where our spirit or soul has its reality, this is where the *Power of Thought* and *Visualization* are supreme. The real you (soul / spirit / higher self) is perfect and free from all illness. We are spirit, although while on earth we also have a physical presence. Our body in this life is like the clothes we put on when we get up in the morning, but at the end of the day (when we die), we discard these clothes. The next day, when we are reborn (reincarnated), we put on different clothes, but as spirit, we remain the same. Some of the things we have learned in this life are carried over with us into the next life, and we keep coming back until we reach the stage of perfection, after which there is no need for us to get dressed (reincarnated) as we can now stay in the real realm of perfection.

Visualization in meditation can bring about this communication with your real self (soul / spirit). By using imagination, we are sending a message to our subconscious. The old adage "Be careful what you wish for" is very true. When we visualize, we must be clear about what we want, and it should not be used to harm to others. You may want a better job or you may want to find the ideal partner, but it is important you don't put faces to the partner or friend whom you want to attract. Your "higher self" knows what is right for you. So, if you are ill, you should visualize yourself becoming closer to your "real self", which, as we have already seen, is perfect and free from sickness and pain.

Understanding the Techniques

The Placebo Effect

The placebo effect is the power of the mind to influence the body. It is how our expectations and beliefs can bring a *real* change in our physical and mental well-being.

In the late nineteen sixties, just before I started my long career in the Royal Navy, I worked as a barman in Dublin. The pub was called the "Cutty Sark", and it was situated on Ellis Quay by the river Liffey. At that time, the area around Benburb Street and Smithfield was one of deprivation and poverty, so this was one of those pubs that could be found in any similar area of Liverpool or Glasgow.

The majority of the customers came from the same background. Women were not allowed in the bar area and had to drink in the snug: and anyway, women did not go into a pub on their own unless they were "ladies of the night". It was not unusual for men to come straight in from work and carry on drinking till closing time, and these were what you might call seasoned drinkers. One busy Friday night, one of the regulars who I will call Mike was having his usual whiskey and lemonade. (In Ireland, we have what is called red lemonade.) As the evening progressed Mike was enjoying the company of his fellow drinkers and sooner or later, he would reach the stage that I call falling-down drunk.

It was acceptable for a man to get drunk in our bar, but if they got drunk in another pub before they came in, they would be refused service. In one of the pubs where I worked, the bar counter stretched right across the room, from one wall to the lounge area. One day, a drunk came in through the bar door, and I refused to serve him. A few minutes later, he came in through the lounge door, and again, I refused to serve him. In frustration, he exclaimed loudly, ' how many f***ing pubs do you work in!'

One of the requirements for a barman in the Cutty Sark was the ability to jump over the bar and eject troublemakers. Some of the pubs had a raised area behind the bar to give the impression of extra height to the staff. (There were no barmaids in Dublin in those days: it was a purely male environment).

Returning to that Friday night, Mike was getting close to the falling-down stage. He was a little fellow who worked as a dustbin man for the Dublin Corporation, and he was a popular man who never caused any trouble. To carry on drinking would have been a waste of his money and whiskey, but refusing to serve him might mean he'd take offence and take his future custom elsewhere. I decided to carry on serving him, but when he ordered his whiskey and red lemonade, he only got the lemonade part of the drink. He carried on drinking and showed the effects that would be expected were he drinking whiskey and not just lemonade!

The next day when he came, in I told him what I had done and gave him the money he would have saved by not having the whiskey in his drink, but for some strange reason, I don't think he appreciated what I had done. Working as a barman in the some of the poorest areas of Dublin had a profound effect on my life. Night after night, I saw men drinking while their wives and

Understanding the Techniques

children went hungry, and this was the main reason for me leaving the bar trade. However, the point of this tale was to demonstrate the way that Mike's mind believed he was still getting the effects of the whiskey, even when it was absent from his drink.

I wrote the following poem to express my feelings about that time in my life.

Unrewarded Youth

They watched the mist as it drifted
Along the dark deserted quay.
In the distance they heard the sound
Of departing ships.
The girl aged twelve and the boy aged four,
Stood waiting at the bar room door.
The smoke, the light, the noise and din,
Echoed from the crowd within.
Inside the pub they could hear,
Their father's voice above the cackle of
Good cheer as they toasted each other
With pints of beer.
In the shadows they did wait, grey and
Disgruntled as the hour grew late.
When at last he did appear, his step
Unsteady, his eyes unclear.
He bid his children take his hand and lead
Him home through this dirty depressing land.
Its lofty tenements damp and dim
With all the misery that dwelt within.

Chapter 6:
Healing the Past

Healing the past is important if we are to free ourselves, and allow ourselves to live to our full potential of a happy and healthy life. Some past issues can be buried so deeply that we don't admit to ourselves that they exist. Childhood trauma can be both physical and mental. As children, we depend on our parents and others in authority to protect and love us. When they let us down, it leaves a wound that remains open, and we carry this pain through our life like a heavy weight within our being.

There can be many causes for these past wounds; children who lose a parent at an early age may feel they are being punished, so self-blame is a common symptom of these historical events. We must first bring the cause into the open and accept that it needs to be healed, then we can send healing to the time when problem arose. You might say, "How can we send healing to the past?" because after all, the past has already happened. It is easier if we look at the past, present and future as three lines running alongside each in parallel rather than in a linear form, as this makes it much easier to access the past by crossing from one line to another, rather than travelling back in time.

Healing the Past

We can also carry things requiring healing from previous reincarnations. A friend of mine had a recurring dream of being crucified. This always started with her looking up to a star filled sky, and then, while she was on the cross, a Roman centurion would break her legs with a metal bar. She complained of having pains in her lower legs in this life, and she put this down to the fact that she did a lot of horse riding, but the pains could have been caused or exacerbated by the previous life experience of having her legs deliberately smashed by the centurion. We associate crucifixion as being nailed to a cross, but this was not always the case, as sometimes the person being executed would be attached to the cross with ropes, and a footrest attached to the cross, for the purpose of taking the person's weight off the wrists. Sometimes this can be seen in representations of the crucifixion of Jesus. I explained that it was a tradition to break the legs of the person being crucified when they were hung on the cross, to prevent them being untied and escaping.

The typical crucifixion lasted several days, with the person raising him or herself up to breathe, and then slumping back down again, owing to the effort this required and the pain it caused. When the person slumped back down, he struggled to breathe, and as his strength ran out, he slowly suffocated. Needless to say, thirst also played a part, although not hunger, as we tend not to feel hunger when in severe pain and distress.

The way to heal this kind of trauma from a past life is to forgive those who did us harm and also to ask for forgiveness for the wrongs we may have done during our previous lifetime.

Do You Really Want To Be Healed?

The Healing

The success of healing depends on a combination of conditions, including the skill of the healer and the openness of the person receiving the healing. For instance, the fact that you have read my book up to this point, is an indication that you want to be healed, and the next step is to believe that you can be healed. We start with the belief that, "Everyone is entitled to be happy", and indeed, you are here to be healthy and happy. The real you is free from all forms of illness, whether it be physical or emotional, so you must connect to that real self and allow the mind to begin the process of healing.

There is a true story of a woman who had cancer, and who had been told by the doctors that she would soon die. She went to a psychic surgeon, who performed a healing upon her and told her she had been healed, but she had no faith in the fact that she had been healed and she died soon after. At her autopsy, they found no sign of the cancer. She had been healed, but her perception was that the psychic healing had not worked, so her death became her reality.

Therefore, you must want to be healed and you must be prepared to accept the outcome. When you say, "I want to be healed," you are implying that healing is needed and are willing to accept that healing, and your desire to be healed will lead you to the person or place that will facilitate the healing.

Healing the Past

*"Every good act is an opening through which
the Light of God shines"*

Chapter 7:
Reiki, or Energy Healing

We are surrounded by energy. Our body is made up of electromagnetic energy. But there is also the energy we get from our environment; such as the trees we see, the wind we feel, the air we breathe, even from the earth we stand on. Another type of energy is the energy we get from the divine or universal life force. If you are religious, you may use the words Holy Spirit or God for the source of this energy, but you don't have to believe in God to receive Reiki healing, because Reiki is not connected to any religion.

The Usui Reiki healer has been attuned by a Reiki master who himself / herself was also attuned by a Reiki master. Reiki training and attunements are passed down from person to person, so that all Reiki masters can trace their lineage back to "Dr. Mikao Usui". For information on how to become a Reiki healer, visit the *UK Reiki Federation* website. Although I said that Reiki is not attached to any religion, I do believe that being a spiritual person does help.

The UK Reiki Federation provides the following information for clients and patients:

Reiki, or Energy Healing

What is Reiki

Reiki is a natural healing energy that is activated by intention. It works on every level, and not just the physical. As we mentioned earlier, the practice of Reiki is an original method of healing developed by Dr. Mikao Usui in Japan in the 20th Century.

The Benefits of Reiki

Illness can be a time of great stress, and Reiki can help us cope by encouraging relaxation and bringing balance to both mind and emotions. People who have received a Reiki treatment have said that they felt a deep relaxation that promotes a calm, peaceful sense of well-being on all levels. Reiki also encourages and supports positive personal choices, such as improving diet, taking more exercise, devoting time for rest or leisure activities, and it may reduce the need for alcohol and tobacco. It engenders greater inner harmony and balance. Regular Reiki treatments promote a calmer response to life's challenges. Reiki's gentle energy is easily adapted to most medical conditions and may be used safely by people of all ages, including newborn babies, pregnant mothers, surgical patients, the frail and the elderly.

Safety

Reiki is non-invasive, gentle yet powerful, and it may be used with confidence alongside orthodox health-care. As such, it expands treatment options. Reiki is not an alternative to conventional medicine, so you

Do You Really Want To Be Healed?

should therefore always consult a doctor about any medical, acute or infectious conditions, and for problems of an urgent nature.

What Happens During a Reiki Session?

A Reiki treatment is non-diagnostic, non-interventionist and non-manipulative. No pressure is applied to the body. A session is usually carried out with the recipient lying down or sitting in a comfortable and peaceful environment. There is no need to remove any clothing, as Reiki energy passes easily through all materials. The practitioner places his or her hands gently on or over the body; there is no massage or manipulation. Reiki can also be given over a distance.

Reiki may be experienced as a flow of energy, and the client may experience some mild tingling, warmth, coolness or some other sensation. Alternatively, he or she may feel nothing at all. The length of a Reiki session is usually one hour.

Reiki can release emotional problems that have been lying dormant for years, and that need to be brought to the surface in order to be healed. We may not be comfortable having to face these problems or issues, but they need to come into the open to be healed, otherwise we carry them like a heavy weight in this life, or even into our next reincarnation.

Reiki, or Energy Healing

Prepare for a Reiki session

There are a few things that I would suggest that will enhance your healing:

Refrain from eating meat, fowl or fish for two days before the healing. These foods often contain drugs like penicillin, female hormones and toxins in the form of pesticides and heavy metal, which can make your system sluggish and throw it off balance.

- Consider a water or juice fast the day before treatment, breaking the fast on the morning of treatment.
- Stop or minimise your use of tea and coffee, but drink bottled still water instead.
- Stop drinking alcohol and stop smoking three days prior to healing.
- Stop eating sweets.
- Cut down or stop watching television, listening to the radio and reading newspapers.
- Go for quite walks, spend time with nature and get moderate exercise.
- Meditate for half an hour each day, using a style with which you are familiar, or simply spend the time in silence.
- Release all anger, fear, jealousy, hate and worry and give it up to the light.
- Create a sacred space within and around your-self.

Remember these are only suggestions, so don't worry if you don't use them. The main thing is that you are open to the healing.

Chapter 8:
Other Forms of Holistic Healing

Although I am a Reiki healer, I believe that some people might find other forms of holistic healing more suited to their needs.

Acupuncture is an ancient Chinese therapy that involves inserting needles into the skin at specific points in the body. This form of healing is becoming more popular in the west.

Shiatsu is also a form of energy healing that does involve a certain amount of manipulation and massage. It will help the flow of energy around the body. From personal experience of having a session of Shiatsu, I can recommend it for muscular pain and general well-being.

Reflexology is a technique of diagnosis and treatment in which certain areas of the body, particularly the feet are massaged to alleviate pain or other symptoms in the organs of the body.

Other Forms of Holistic Healing

Anchors and Attachments

You have heard the expression, "Ships that pass in the night". Well, we are like ships sailing through life, visiting some places that are lovely and some that are not. Just like a ship, we need to look after engines or sails. The machinery on a ship not only allows the ship to move, because it also generates electricity which heats and pumps the water around the ship, so it keeps us warm and clean, helps us cook our food and to generally live a comfortable life at sea.

I recall that during the Falklands conflict, the Royal Navy ships in San Carlos Waters (which became known as "Bomb Alley") were taking a battering from the Argentine aircraft. One of the Royal Navy frigates had sustained damage that resulted in the ship being without power, so with only an emergency generator to supply a limited amount of light, the crew set about repairing the damaged machinery. This would take some time to complete, so in the semi darkness without hot food or water, it was decided that some of the crew could be spared to go to the larger ships that were situated outside "Bomb Alley", and get a hot meal and shower before returning to the damaged ship.

The contrast between where they had been and the larger ships was highlighted by the main broadcast, which told the crew that their mail was ready for collection from the mail office, and they could collect their laundry from the Chinese laundry. As you can imagine, they were not looking forward to returning to their own ship and all the hardship and uncertainty that awaited them.

Do You Really Want To Be Healed?

Sometimes life can be like that. We can be in a bad place but at the same time be shown a glimpse of how things can and should be. Those sailors had no choice: they had to return and repair their ship, but with emotional issues, we often *do* have a choice. We can decide whether a situation is worth the effort required to fix it, or whether we should give it up as a bad job and move on. There are always factors that can influence our decision, such as whether our metaphorical ship is going to sink anyway, which means that it is definitely time to leave! Only we can gauge how strong the attachment to the situation is, and only we can work out whether we can break free, and whether there is a better place to go to.

Anchors can keep us safe in times of rough seas, so it is important that they are fixed to something or someone who is solid and supportive. If you want to sail to a better place, you can always take your anchor with you, just as a ship does.

Attachments are things that we decide to cling to. Think of an illness as an attachment, just like the barnacles on the hull of a ship, these can slow you down and make you feel heavy. It does not have to be a particular illness, it might be a person or even a job that is having a negative effect on your life, and making you unhappy. If you wish to carry on with these negative attachments, that is all right, because we all have free will. On the other hand, if you want to get rid of a negative attachment that is causing your illness or emotional problem, remember that you are not on your own. We all have a guardian angel, who is there to help us find the solutions to our problems. Because of free will, you do need to ask

Other Forms of Holistic Healing

for help and the angels don't intervene unless requested to do so. Once you are open to receiving help, you will be surprised how quickly and in what form that help will come to you. You may be led to a better place or person.

The Healer

We all have the ability to heal each other and ourselves. So why are some people better healers then others? To facilitate the healing, I believe you need certain qualities. Two of these qualities are *Love* and *Compassion*. It is easy to love those who are close to us, such as our children, spouses and other family members. This is because we feel that they love us in return, and we all want love in our lives. It takes a bit more practice to love those whom we haven't actually met.

Over the course of time during my own wife's long battle with cancer, she spent many weeks in hospital. There were some nurses who she liked more than others, and it wasn't that they were more competent then the others, it was simply they had something special about them. If you look closely, you will see that many people in the health and care services have that special gift.

It may be just a kind word or gentle touch that makes you feel loved. When we love someone, we want to help and protect them. A good healer will give the same amount of love and compassion to everyone, irrespective of their personal feelings. Every good act is an opening through which the light of God shines.

Do You Really Want To Be Healed?

So each time we practise goodness, we receive a special measure of God's Grace, and it is through the Grace of God that we become better healers.

When a Royal Navy ship used to visit Hong Kong for maintenance periods, the ship's sides were painted by local native women who were known as the "Jenny Side Party". These were mostly small, middle-aged women who wore loose black shirts and trousers, and they were unmarried. These women also went into the boiler and engine rooms of the ship to clean the bilges. The machinery space bilges were not very pleasant places to be, as they were normally filled with black oily water and sludge. It was not the easiest place to clean, because of all the different pipes that criss-cross each other. There is a saying that when a Naval Architect designs a ship, he puts the first pipe in straight, and all the other pipes have to go over and under that first pipe, so it ends up looking like a snake's wedding.

These women would crawl between the pipes in the bilge with a dustpan and bucket, cleaning up without a word of complaint. Very few people were aware that most of the money they earned doing this unpleasant work was used to help the orphan children of Hong Kong. They were performing an act of love and compassion, without any direct contact to those who were benefiting from their love. This is an example of how to give unconditional love.

We have now reached the end of this book, but hopefully it is just the beginning of a life free from the illusion of illness and pain. Remember that *anything can be healed,* if you really want to be healed.

Index

A

Acupuncture 12, 32
affirmations 19
Age of Aquarius 12
Anchors 34
ancient China 3
Anger 5
anger issues 6
anti-depressants 3
anti-depression pills 8
anxiety 9
anything can be healed 36
Astral Level 16
Attachments 34
Aura 16
Aura, final 16
Aura, first 16
Aura, fourth 16
Aura, second 16
Aura, third 16

B

Benburb Street 21
Bible stories 1

blockage 15
Body, Etheric Auric 16
Body, Physical Auric 16
Body, Vital Auric 16
Bomb Alley 33
Buddhist sacred texts 2

C

Chakra, Brow 14
Chakra, Crown 13, 14, 15
Chakra, Heart 13, 15
Chakra, Root 15
Chakra, Root/Base 10, 14, 15
Chakra, Sacral 9, 15
Chakra, Solar Plexus 6, 15
Chakra, Spleen 14
Chakra, Third Eye 14, 15
Chakra, Throat 15
Chakras, lower 15
Chi 11
cholesterol-lowering statins 3
coal delivery man 10
Compassion 35
cosmos 12
crucifixion 25
Cutty Sark 21, 22

D

depression 9
Dublin, growing up in 8

E

energy 11
energy, electromagnetic 28

Index

F
Falklands conflict 33
five principles 5

G
Greater Reality 19

H
healing 26
higher self 15
Holistic approach 3
Hong Kong 36

I
isolation 9

J
Jenny Side Party 36

K
Ki 11, 15

L
Love 35
Lower Mental / Divine Level 17

M
Meditation 18
meditation, Christian 18
Meridian system 15
Mike 21, 22
Mount Kurama 2

N
nation of hypochondriacs 3

Do You Really Want To Be Healed?

NHS 3

P
placebo effect 21
Power of Thought 20
Prana 11
psychic surgeon 26
psychological illnesses 9

R
Reflexology 32
regular prescription drugs 3
Rei 11
Rei-Ki 11
Reiki practitioner's code 5
Reiki treatment 30
Reiki, Benefits of 29
Roman centurion 25

S
Safety 29
San Carlos Waters 33
satori 2
Shiatsu 32
Stoker Petty Officer 19
Stress 5
stress, root cause of 19
superheated steam 19

T
Taff 12
Third Eye 14
Throat 14

Index

U

UK Reiki Federation 28
universal life force 28
Unrewarded Youth 23
Usui Reiki 28
Usui, Dr. Mikao 1, 28, 29

V

Visualization 19, 20

W

What if 7
wheel 14
Worry 5, 7

Stellium Ltd

We hope that you enjoyed reading this book.

It would be helpful to other prospective readers if you would kindly leave a review on Amazon.

For news of more new titles similar to this one, please visit www.stelliumpub.com from time to time, or email us at stelliumpub@gmail.com

Lightning Source UK Ltd.
Milton Keynes UK
UKHW021256020120
356168UK00007B/1240/P